At school

CD

WB

That´s me

What is your name?

This is my school

Hallo ihr,
Jch heiße Lisa Melzer und wohne mit meinen Eltern seit einem Jahr in London. Mein Dad arbeitet hier bei einer deutschen Firma. Jch gehe zur Woodford Green Primary School in der Nähe von Epping Forest. Wir tragen hier alle eine Schuluniform. Unser Unterricht fängt um 9.00 Uhr an und dauert bis 15.30 Uhr. Jeden Mittwoch und Freitag haben wir eine assembly, dann singen wir zusammen, manchmal trägt die drama group etwas vor oder Schüler bekommen für besondere Leistungen einen award. Jn der Mittagspause essen wir gemeinsam in der Schule. Meine Lieblingsfächer sind English, science und P.E. (so nennt man hier den Sportunterricht). Wir haben in unserer Klasse vier Computer. Damit üben wir zum Beispiel lesen und schreiben. Dafür gibt es aber auch tolle computer games!
Gibt es das bei euch in der Schule jetzt auch?

Bye **Lisa**

PS: J can speak English now!

WB

In the classroom

school bag

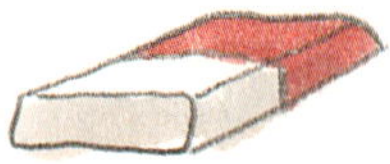
rubber

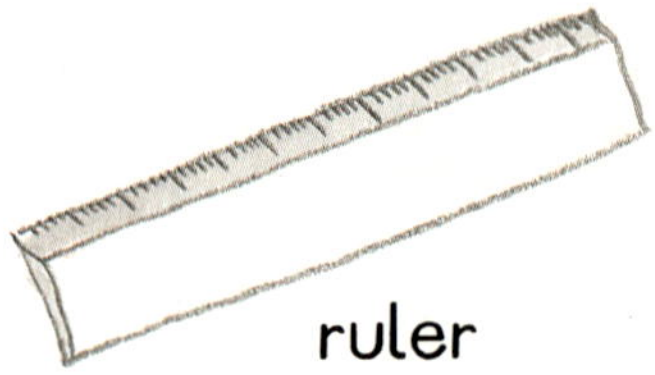
ruler

computer

glue

coloured pencils

lunchbox

book

exercise book

school uniform

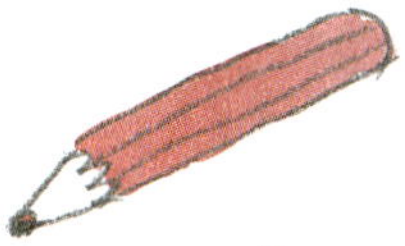
pencil

chair

blackboard

window

door

scissors

pencil case

folder

pens

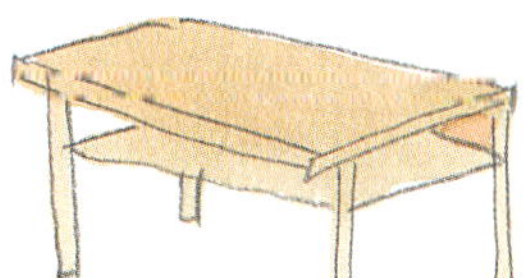
table

CD

School rap

Hey boys and girls!
Let´s go to school.
Let´s read and write.
That´s great, that´s cool.

Hey boys and girls!
Let´s go to school.
Let´s count and draw.
That´s great, that´s cool.

Hey boys and girls!
Let´s go to school.
Let´s sing and play.
That´s great, that´s cool.

 Rap and play!

A friend from Great Britain

CD

Colours and clothes

CD

WB

Our favourite clothes

What colours can you find in the picture?

What are your favourite clothes?

CD
WB

A fashion show at school

What are they wearing?

Have a fashion show in your class.

Hits for kids

Hot summer hits *Winter fashion news*

What do you like for summer? What do you like for winter?

Hi Max,

heute war ich mit Mama shoppen. Jch brauche nämlich neue Anziehsachen für die Schule. Nein, keine neuen jeans or trainers, sondern eine Schuluniform! Wusstest du, dass man hier in den meisten Schulen school uniforms tragen muss? Es gibt dafür sogar extra shops und Abteilungen in den großen Kaufhäusern. Manchmal haben Mädchen wie die Jungs Schulkrawatten um. Die meisten Schulen haben sogar ihr eigenes Schulwappen. Das heißt school badge und wird auf die pullovers and jackets genäht. Was sagst du dazu? Jch finde es really cool. Jetzt muss ich morgens nicht mehr überlegen, was ich anziehen soll. Unsere Lehrerin sagt, dass es in vielen anderen Ländern wie Jtalien oder der Türkei auch Schuluniformen gibt. Frag doch mal Songül, ob das stimmt!

Take care **Lisa**

PS: That`s me and my friends in our school uniforms:

Clothes that protect us

WB

What do the children need for their sports?

Let us play

CD

WB

School playground games

How many games can you find?

What games can you play?

CD

WB

Teddy bear, teddy bear

Teddy bear, teddy bear,
Turn around.
Teddy bear, teddy bear,
Touch the ground.

Teddy bear, teddy bear,
Shake your head.
Teddy bear, teddy bear,
Go to bed.

Teddy bear, teddy bear,
Jump the stairs.
Teddy bear, teddy bear,
Eat some pears.

Teddy bear, teddy bear,
Turn out the light.
Teddy bear, teddy bear,
Say "Good night".

Rap and play!

Outdoor game

Hello Melanie,
Many thanks for the card. Bei uns in der Schule war letzte Woche ein "Games Day".
That was fun! Einen Tag lang haben wir die tollsten Spiele gespielt. Das war mein absolutes Lieblingsspiel. Super cool! Wir spielen es nun immer in der Pause: Catch the Dragon´s Tail!
Wir stellen uns hintereinander und halten uns am Vordermann fest.
Die erste Person ist der Kopf des Drachens, der Letzte ist der Schwanz.
Der Kopf versucht nun den Schwanz zu fangen. Ein Spaß für die Leute in der Mitte, die nicht wissen, wohin es geht! Hat der Kopf den Drachenschwanz gefangen, wird ausgewechselt und das Spiel beginnt aufs Neue.

Do you like the game?
Bye Lisa

Games, games, games

Which games do you know?

Which games can you play with a partner?

Classroom games

CD

Play the games!

Animals

CD

WB

Farm animals

What animals live on a farm?

What animals do you like?

How to draw a dog

Try to draw a dog with your partner.

Can you draw Bumblebee?

Down on the farm

Down on the farm at the end of the day
All the animals politely say:
Thank you for treating us kindly today.
Thank you dear farmer this is what we say:

CD

Listen and play.

Baby animals

CD

WB

WB

Our pets

Make an animal poster.

Hi Melissa,

wir haben mit meiner Klasse einen Ausflug nach Dartmoor gemacht. Damit du siehst, wo das ist: Dartmoor ist ein großes Moor. Really scary! Aber das Tollste

sind die zotteligen Dartmoor Ponies, die hier noch wild leben und frei umher-laufen. Das ganze Jahr über! Jmmer wieder sind wir kleinen Herden begegnet. Unsere Lehrerin meint, wir dürften sie aber nicht füttern. Sonst gewöhnen sie sich an Menschen und laufen auf die Straße, wo sie überfahren wer-den. Auch streicheln sollten wir sie nicht, denn manchmal können sie auch beißen. Dabei sind sie so superniedlich. Schade, dass ich kein Pony haben kann. What do you think?

See you soon Lisa

Animal rap

CD

I have got a hamster. You have got a cat.

Sue has got a budgie. Tom has got a rat.

Sue loves her . Tom his .

We our animals. We our pets.
We our animals. We our pets.

My eats carrots, my likes mice.
My drinks water, my eats rice.

 Do the rap.

Sports and action

CD

WB

At the gym

What is your favourite sport?

Can you play the P. E. teacher?

CD

WB

Sports on TV

What are they talking about? Listen and point.

Hi Lindiwe,

zweimal in der Woche haben wir in der Schule nachmittags P.E. Das heißt physical education, so nennt man hier den Sportunterricht. Dabei habe ich ein Spiel kennen gelernt, das in Deutschland keiner spielt. Es heißt cricket. Leider ist es super schwer zu erklären. Auch die Erwachsenen spielen cricket und es gibt sogar Länderspiele, zum Beispiel mit Australien, Pakistan und Jndien! Zwei Teams mit je elf Spielern spielen manchmal fünf Tage lang gegeneinander. Cricket wird in ganz weißer Kleidung gespielt. Der bat sieht aus wie ein platter Baseballschläger, also so:

Am lustigsten sieht aber der Schiedsrichter aus! Er trägt einen langen weißen Kittel. Jch habe erst gedacht er wäre ein Arzt!

How are you doing? Was gibt`s Neues aus eurem Sportunterricht?

See you Lisa

At the sports shop

CD

WB

What would you like to buy?

What are the things for?

Birthday

CD

Birthday at school

Dear Songül,
Many thanks for your birthday card. Gestern war es toll in der Schule. Wir hatten assembly in der Aula und der Rektor Mr Snow rief mich plötzlich auf die Bühne. Hatte ich etwas angestellt!? Doch dann sah ich das Tablett mit den vielen Geschenken – mein Herz machte einen Sprung, denn nun wusste ich, dass wir meinen Geburtstag feiern! Lustig wurde es, als alle Kinder versuchten mir auf deutsch zu gratulieren. Jch musste "Herzlichen Glückwunsch" vier mal vorsagen! Dann hat die ganze Schule "Happy birthday to you" gesungen. Jch habe ein Geschenk ausgesucht und später im Klassenraum ausgepackt. Jt was a pink piggy bank! Really sweet!

Love from **Lisa**
PS: J'm having a birthday party this afternoon, and the weather is super and sunny. Hurrah! PPS: J wish you were here.

Happy birthday!

WB

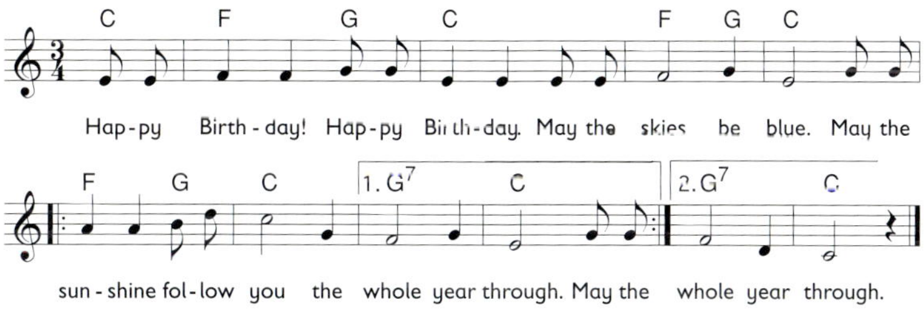

Happy birthday, happy birthday to a very special friend,
happy birthday dear Lisa, best wishes we send!

Dear Lisa, dear Lisa, it´s your birthday today,
Let´s clap now for Lisa. Let´s sing out hooray!

Do you understand the wishes?

CD

Have a doughnut!

Party games

Have a birthday party in your class!

Shopping

CD

WB

At the shopping centre

What can you buy at the shops?

What can you see in the trolley?

CD
WB

No T-shirt for Simon?

How many pounds has Simon got?

Can you help Simon?

Hi Linda,
Gestern habe ich das erste Mal englisches pocket money bekommen. Meine Eltern gaben mir £ 2.50. Zuerst war ich unheimlich enttäuscht, weil es so wenig war. Aber dann haben meine Eltern mir erklärt, dass es genauso viel Taschengeld ist wie in Deutschland.
£ steht für pound. Ein £ besteht aus 100 pence. Das wird "p" abgekürzt. Ein "p" heißt übrigens penny, mehrere nennt man pence.
Jch habe also 2 pounds 50 pence Taschengeld bekommen. Die Hälfte davon habe ich sofort in meine piggy bank gesteckt – ich spare nämlich für ein super cooles T-shirt! Do you have a piggy bank too?
With love
Lisa

WB At the fruit and vegetable Shop

What would you like to buy?

Healthy food

CD

 to bite, 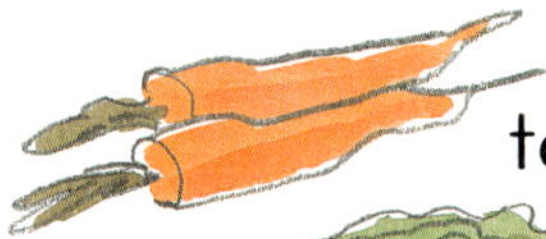 to crunch,

  and  to munch.

 to nibble, 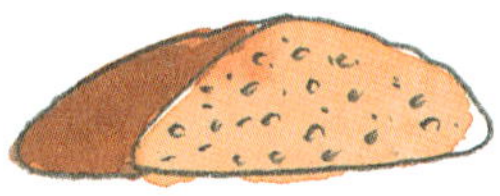 to chew,

and 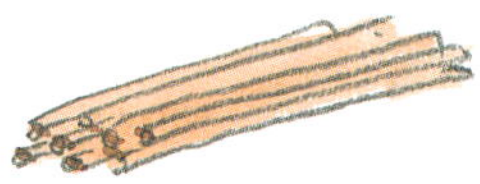 too.

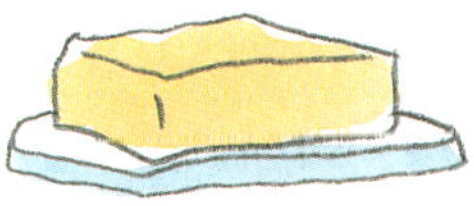

  and  all keep us healthy.

So that is what we eat!

Try to read the healthy food rhyme.

Apples and bananas

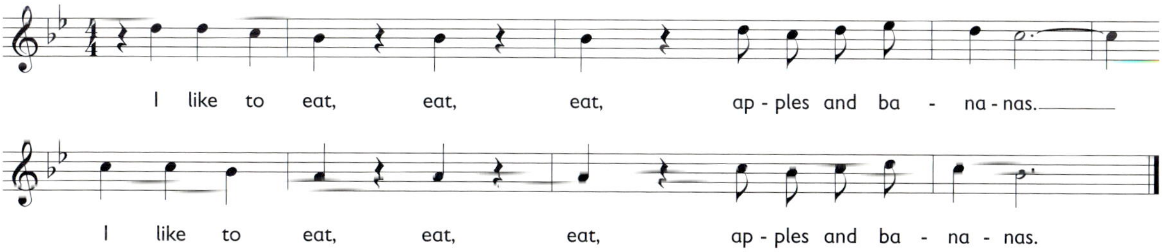

CD

Can you think of another verse?

Dragons

CD WB

Bumbleebee´s new friend

Bumblebee! What a mess!
It was Nessie!
Where is Nessie?
She has gone!
Don't cry, Bumblebee.
Will Nessie come back?
Bumblebee Times

Nessie´s photo album

Loch Ness

Edinburgh Castle

knights

playing the bagpipes

the Scottish Highlands

Highland cows

sheep

Highland Games

Hello Max,
glaubst du, dass es in Schottland noch Ungeheuer gibt? J don`t! Wir waren letzte Woche auf Klassenfahrt in Edinburgh, das ist die Hauptstadt von Schottland. Wir haben dort das castle besichtigt und die crown jewels gesehen! Am letzten Tag haben wir einen Ausflug nach Loch Ness gemacht. Du weißt schon, da wohnt das Seeungeheuer Nessie.
Man glaubt, dass ein riesiges Reptil seit der letzten Eiszeit auf dem Grund des unheimlich tiefen Sees lebt und manchmal auftaucht. Really scary!!! Du kannst im Jnternet alles darüber lesen und mit einer webcam nach Nessie suchen.
Viele Männer tragen in Schottland kilts, das sind Röcke aus dem karierten Schottenstoff. That`s funny, isn`t it? Jeder Familien-Clan hat sein eigenes Muster. Stell dir vor, es gibt über 600 eingetragene Schottenmuster.
Lustig sind auch die Dudelsackspieler. Man hört und sieht sie fast überall in Schottland. Jch habe auch versucht, auf den bagpipes zu spielen, aber ich habe keinen Ton herausbekommen!

Bye **Lisa**

Postman Pete

CD

WB

Here comes the postman

Here comes our Postman Pete
All dressed in blue.
Has he got a letter
For me or for you?

He carries his postbag
Through sunshine, rain or snow.
Brings letters, postcards, parcels
And always says hello.

He knows a lot of people
In our little town:
The baker, the policeman
Mr Potter and Miss Brown.

Here comes our Postman Pete
All dressed in blue.
Has he got a letter
For me or for you?

Who does Pete know?

Describe Postman Pete.

A postman at work

It is 5 a.m.
Pete arrives at the post office.

Pete sorts out the letters.

Then he packs his bag.

Pete gets his bicycle.

He delivers the post.

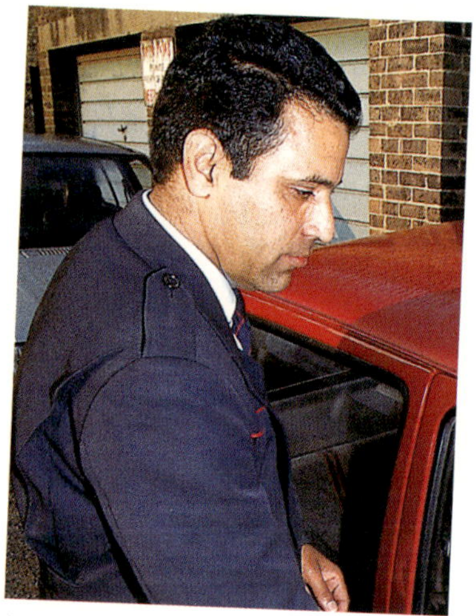

It is 1 p.m.
Pete drives home.

What do you know about Pete´s working day?

What about your postman´s working day?

At the post office

Act it out.

Hello Julia,
am Wochenende war ich mit meinen Eltern im Post Office Museum in Bath. Mein Dad ist nämlich Briefmarkensammler. Hast du dir schon einmal Briefmarken genauer angesehen? Auf jeder Briefmarke muss eigentlich der Name des Landes stehen, in dem sie gültig ist. Nur Großbritannien macht eine Ausnahme. Hier reicht ein Bild – meist ein Portrait der Königin – und der Wert der Marke. Das ist so, weil die Briten 1840 die ersten waren, die Briefmarken druckten. Jch sammle jetzt übrigens auch stamps. Ein paar davon schicke ich dir mit!
Love **Lisa**

PS: Can you send me some stamps?

Days, weeks and months

CD

WB

Around the year

Play the season game.

What belongs to winter?

CD

WB

My busy day

I have breakfast.

I play in the garden.

I go shopping.

I have tea.

I watch TV.

I go to bed.

What is your day like?

Do you know Peter McFrundy?

CD
WB

Every week Peter McFrundy
Has got crafts at school on Monday.

He plays football on Tuesday
And makes music on Wednesday.

He surfs the web on Thursday
And goes jogging on Friday.

He goes swimming on Saturday
And makes the breakfast on Sunday.

Well, that is the week of Peter McFrundy.

Listen and find the right pictures.

What is your week like?

CD WB

Lisa´s timetable

Woodford Green Primary School **Timetable**
name: Lisa Melzer

Time	Monday	Tuesday	Wednesday	Thursday	Friday
9.00-10.00	**English**	**maths**	**English**	**maths**	**English**
10.00-10.45	break	break	assembly/ break	break	assembly/ break
10.45-12.30	**maths**	**English**	**maths**	**English**	**maths**
12.30-13.30	lunch break	lunch break	lunch break	lunch break	lunch break
13.30-15.30	**science art**	**IT history**	**music PE**	**geography RE**	**science music**

IT=information technology RE=religious education PE=physical education

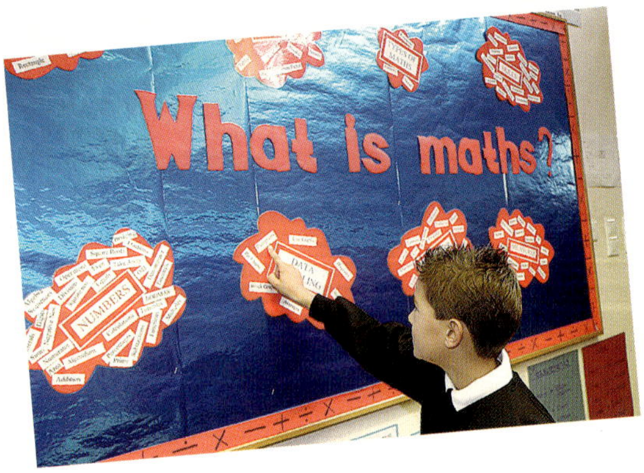

What are Lisa´s subjects?

What is your favourite subject at school?

Hi Kevin,
Schule in England ist doch ganz anders als in Deutschland. Guck mal auf meinen timetable. Da kannst du sehen, welchen Unterricht ich habe. Wir haben jeden Vormittag Englisch and maths. That`s really hard work! Das beste daran sind natürlich die langen Pausen. Mittwochs und Freitags haben wir mit der ganzen Schule assembly. Davon habe ich dir ja schon erzählt, weißt du noch? Mittags haben wir von 12.30-13.30 Uhr lunch break. Da esse ich mit den anderen Kindern zusammen in der Schulkantine. Das ist lustig, aber es schmeckt nie so gut wie zu Hause bei Mum.
Da fällt mir ein: Gestern ist mir etwas Witziges passiert! Meine Lehrerin wollte meine Mum um 8.00 Uhr in der Schule sprechen. Mum hat komisch geguckt, denn die Schule beginnt ja erst um 9.00 Uhr. Als wir ankamen, war die Schule noch abgeschlossen und ganz dunkel. Um halb neun kam meine Lehrerin Mrs Brown. Die war überrascht, dass Mum schon da war! Die beiden haben ganz schön gelacht, weil ich vergessen hatte, dass man in England „8 a.m." oder „8 p.m." sagt. Das sind Abkürzungen für die lateinischen Bezeichnungen „ante meridiem" für vor dem Mittag und „post meridiem" für nach dem Mittag.
How are you doing? Can you speak English now too? Please write me soon!!
Take care **Lisa**

Christmas

CD

WB

A letter to Father Christmas

What are your wishes for Christmas?

What are Pussy´s wishes?

Waiting for Christmas

CD
WB

Do you like the Christmas decorations?

How many presents are there?

CD
WB

Christmas Day

 What has everybody got?

 What about your presents for your family?

 Mime an angel, a Christmas tree, a turkey ...

Dear Nele,
weißt du was, wir feiern dieses Jahr englische Weihnachten. Und das geht so: Schon eine Woche vor Weihnachten schmücken wir den Christmas tree. Am 24. Dezember, also Christmas Eve, hängen wir unsere stockings an den Kamin. In der Nacht kommt dann Father Christmas mit seinem Schlitten durch den chimney und bringt die Geschenke. Alles, was zu groß für die stockings ist, legt er natürlich unter den Weihnachtsbaum!
Der nächste Tag ist Christmas Day. Dann packen wir unsere Geschenke aus und feiern eine riesige Party mit unseren Freunden. Am meisten freue ich mich auf die crackers. Die sehen so  aus. Zwei Leute ziehen daran und mit einem Knall reißt der cracker auseinander und es fallen lustige Sachen heraus: sweets, jokes und ein witziger Papierhut. Und dann geht die Party los!
Merry Christmas and a Happy New Year!
Love **Lisa**

CD
WB

A visit from Father Christmas

Do you get Christmas presents?
No, I don't.
I take presents to children all over the world.
Wow, that is a lot of work.
Please stay for a cup of tea!
Very kind of you. But Rudolph is waiting for me. Merry Christmas!
Merry Christmas to you too! Bye, bye.

Children from Europe

Where are the children from? What do they like?

Bumblebee 3

Textbook (Schülerbuch)
3. Schuljahr

Erarbeitet von
Janice Bland
Ursula Michailow-Drews
Gisela Schultz-Steinbach
Monika Rohletter
Hildegard Thielen
Anne-Katrin Zeich-Pelsis

Zusatzmaterialien:

- Workbook 3 (3-507-02562-0)
- Workbook 3 mit CD (3-507-02564-7)
- Audio-CD (3-507-02568-x)
- Teacher´s Manual 3 (3-507-02566-3)
- Handpuppe (3-507-02530-2)
- Fremdsprachen in der Grundschule – Grundlagen und Praxisbeispiele (3-507-34054-2)
- Fremdsprachen in der Grundschule – Geschichten erzählen im Anfangsunterricht – Storytelling (3-507-34055-0)

ISBN 3-507-02560-4

Druck A 5 4 3 2 1 / Jahr 2006 05 04 03

Alle Drucke der Serie A sind im Unterricht parallel verwendbar, da bis auf die Behebung von Druckfehlern untereinander unverändert.
Die letzte Zahl bezeichnet das Jahr dieses Druckes.

Illustrationen: Klaus Puth
Umschlaggestaltung: Petra Kerker
Satz und Repro: Jürgen Rohrssen, Hannover
Druck: Appl, Wemding

Bildquellen:

S. 5; 14; 54; 55	© Studio Schmidt-Lohmann
S. 30	© dpa. Deutsche Presse-Agentur GmbH. Bilddatenbank
S. 44; 45	© Martin Schindewolf
S. 48	aus: A DAY IN THE LIFE OF A POSTMAN. First published in the UK by Franklin Watts in 1996, a division of The Watts Publishing Group Limited, 96 Leonard Street, London EC2A 4XD.

Textrechte:

S. 33	"Happy Birthday!" 1. Strophe und Melodie: © Terry Kluytmans, KIDiddles, PO Box 52006, Sidney BC V8L 5V9 Canada.